The Longest Night

Written by Jacqueline Guest
Illustrated by Alan Marks

Published by Pearson Education Limited,
80 Strand, London, WC2R 0RL.

www.pearsonschools.co.uk

Text © Pearson Education Limited 2017

Original illustrations © Pearson Education Limited
Illustrated by Alan Marks

First published in the USA by Pearson Education Inc, 2016
First published in the UK by Pearson Education Ltd, 2017

21 20
10 9 8 7

British Library Cataloguing in Publication Data
A catalogue record for this book is available from the British Library

ISBN 978 0 435 18568 8

Copyright notice
All rights reserved. No part of this publication may be reproduced in any form or by any means (including photocopying or storing it in any medium by electronic means and whether or not transiently or incidentally to some other use of this publication) without the written permission of the copyright owner, except in accordance with the provisions of the Copyright, Designs and Patents Act 1988 or under the terms of a licence issued by the Copyright Licensing Agency, Barnards Inn, 86 Fetter Lane, London, EC4A 1EN (www.cla.co.uk). Applications for the copyright owner's written permission should be addressed to the publisher.

Printed in China by Golden Cup

Contents

CHAPTER ONE
Dancing and Dogs — 4

CHAPTER TWO
The Ceremony — 8

CHAPTER THREE
The Journey Begins — 13

CHAPTER FOUR
The First Night — 24

CHAPTER FIVE
The Second Night — 30

CHAPTER SIX
The Longest Night — 38

CHAPTER ONE
Dancing and Dogs

Every eye was on me, Wind Runner of the mighty Raven People, as I danced to the beat of the sacred drum. This was my night. Tomorrow, I would start the most important journey of my life, my Vision Quest, and when I returned from three nights in the wilderness alone, I would be a warrior. At fourteen summers, I would be a man.

The light from the ceremonial fire flashed off the bright red glass beads on my regalia. I'd convinced my mother to trade five rich beaver pelts with the chief trader at the Hudson's Bay post for those beads. The pelts were worth thirty-five knives, but I didn't care. I wanted those beads. My breastplate, which fitted snugly over my buckskin shirt, had a complicated design woven of bone and dyed porcupine quills, and the red beads

made it more beautiful than any other in the tribe.

Whirling and spinning, I leapt high into the air and finished on the last beat of the drum. Everyone cheered and I waved proudly.

Caught up in the excitement, I didn't notice the old mangy dog lurking in the shadows. As I left the dance arena, I stumbled over the animal and fell into the dirt. Instantly angry at being made to look foolish, I stood and shouted at the flea-bitten creature. The dog barked at me, unafraid, before dodging out of my way. My exit was followed by laughter from the crowd and I felt my face flame.

That night, as I carefully packed my dance regalia away, I forgot the humiliating incident with the mangy dog and concentrated on tomorrow. I was sure it would be a triumph for me.

CHAPTER TWO
The Ceremony

I awoke at dawn, excited about the sweat lodge ceremony that would prepare me for my successful Vision Quest. I dressed in only a loincloth and walked to the lodge.

The hides covering the sweat lodge were buffalo – the most important of all the animals Creator had given his people. From this beast, we received the gifts of food, clothing, tools and shelter.

I waited outside as the Shaman chanted a prayer, then lit sweetgrass and sage in a bowl. He used his sacred eagle feather to waft the sweet smoke over me. Once this cleansing smudge was finished, I entered the lodge.

Kneeling, I crawled inside and moved to the left of the opening. The dim light showed me the waiting Elder sitting across from the door. There was a shallow pit in the middle of the floor into which red-hot stones would be placed. Water would be poured over the stones to create steam. The light loincloth I wore would help keep me cool, as it would soon be sweltering inside the lodge.

"Are you prepared for this journey?" Many Horses, the Elder leading the ceremony, asked.

"I am, Grandfather." Although he was not my true relative, I used the term out of respect for this ancient man and his wisdom. "I welcome the trial of the steam and the blessing of the smoke from the sacred herbs."

The Elder nodded approval. "That is good. We need strong warriors for the Raven People."

I boldly went on. "I will tell Creator to send me a fitting Spirit Helper to guide me on my Vision Quest – a cougar perhaps, to show my leadership, or an elk to represent my strength."

When Many Horses spoke, it was as though he were talking to a small child.

"You, Wind Runner, do not tell Creator what Spirit Helper you want. If you deserve one at all, he will send what he thinks you need most for your life journey."

His words made me uncomfortable, as if I should feel shame for speaking my mind. Without thinking, my hand went to my left leg where an ugly red scar ran from my knee to my ankle. A reminder of another time I had been shamed.

When I was twelve, I'd been chased up a tree by a huge grizzly bear. The bear had reached up and scraped my leg with its claws before disappearing into the woods. I'd been so frightened that I had clung to the tree and cried like a small child. It was there, high in the branches, where my father and the other warriors had found me weeping. Even now, as I prepared to join their ranks, the memory haunted me.

CHAPTER THREE
The Journey Begins

After the ceremony in which I bravely endured all four rounds of increasing heat, I spent the rest of the day preparing for what lay ahead. On my Vision Quest, I could take no food, only a skin bag of water. And I would not sleep for three days and nights.

During the nights, I must sit within the sacred circle made from my hand-chosen, dazzling white rocks, which I would carry up the mountainside. If I left the circle, I would fail the test.

The next morning, I stood as the Shaman bestowed the final blessing for my journey. It was a perfect day. The brilliant sunshine shimmered as I admired the beautifully painted teepees, each with its own family design. The entire village had come to wish me luck, including the old dog that had tripped me up.
I glared at it, but the animal must have been too foolish to recognise my warning.

The Shaman finished his blessing, which included asking for help from the rocks I was taking with me – rocks we call Grandfather and Grandmother. Then he leaned in and spoke quietly. "You do not have to go far up the mountain, Wind Runner. For many years, warriors have used a clearing along the trail for this ritual. You will know it when you see it."

"Thank you, but *I* will choose the place for my Vision Quest," I said confidently.

The Shaman raised his eyebrow. "May you find wisdom."

Leaving the village, I began my journey. As I climbed the path up the side of the mountain, I quickly realised that the stones I'd brought to make my circle may not have been the wisest choice. They were heavy, and felt heavier the higher I went. But because they had been blessed, I could not throw them away.

The sun was high when I came to the spot the Shaman had spoken of. I could tell from the fire pit and teepee ring, plus the small stream nearby for water, that this was where other quests had taken place. However, the clearing was barely halfway up the mountain and not impressive at all.

"This is no place for a warrior like me!" I scoffed. "I will climb to the very top for my Vision Quest." I shouted this to the sky and my words were thrown back in my face as they echoed off the steep sides of the mountains.

A rustling sound made me whirl around. "Who's there?" I nervously dropped my hide bag. "I have a bow and arrows . . . and a sharp knife!" None of which I had, but whatever was lurking in the shadows didn't know that.

I tensed, waiting.

Suddenly, a matted brown head poked out from between the bushes, and then the rest of the mangy dog appeared.

"You! You nasty flea-bitten bag of bones! Did you come to embarrass me again?" I picked up a stick and ran at the dog, trying to frighten it.

The foolish dog thought I was playing. It leapt and bounded around me, barking delightedly.

"Stop that! I don't want you here. Now, *go*!" I threw the stick.

The dog retrieved the branch, laying it at my feet.

"I don't have time to bother with you, Worthless One." Picking up the heavy bag of stones, I strode past the panting mutt.

As I walked, the path became steeper. My back ached from the weight of the rocks and I became very thirsty. I knew I should keep my water for later, but decided a small sip wouldn't hurt. Trudging up the mountain, I continued to drink the water until there was little left.

The sun was hiding behind the peaks when I came to a clearing that overlooked the valley far below. The view was amazing.

"Here is a fitting place to make my Vision Quest." I dropped the bag and sat to rest before setting up camp. I was exhausted already and my trial had only just begun.

After stealing another mouthful of water, I set up my sacred space. I pulled the white stones out of the bag and placed them in a circle in which I could comfortably sit. I made sure I left an opening facing east to welcome the first rays of the sun.

When this was done, I made a lean-to of pine branches and stowed everything I had brought with me under the shelter. This consisted of a water skin (now almost empty), the hide bag for my rocks, a parfleche carrier made from buffalo rawhide in which I had sweetgrass and sage, along with flint and steel to light my smudges.

As evening threw long shadows across the clearing, I prepared for my first vigil. I raised my arms to the sky to sing the power song I'd made up. I would ask Creator for his blessing to make it through the coming night. I hadn't earned the song yet, which was a tribute to a warrior's courage and bravery, but decided that it wouldn't be long before I had.

No sooner had I expelled my first breath when a gravelly howl made me stop. There, sitting with its head raised and baying like a fool, was the old dog. "Worthless One, be quiet! You will offend Creator with that racket."

The dog was either deaf or stubborn, and for the rest of my song its unwanted wailing drowned out my words.

CHAPTER FOUR
The First Night

The night sky was filled with a million lights, as though the eyes of the ancestors were watching. I sat in the middle of my stone circle and waited. Tonight, I was sure I would have the vision that would show me my life's path. I was also confident my Spirit Helper would come. Despite the Elder's scolding, I was expecting an important totem animal which would prove Creator favoured me.

The Worthless One lay outside the circle. It smelled as if it had run into a skunk and then rolled in rotten fish!

"Don't bother me. I am waiting for my Spirit Helper."

The old dog raised its head, peered at me with bleary eyes, and belched loudly, adding to the foul smells surrounding it.

I wrinkled my nose.

As the hours dragged by, I sat impatiently waiting, but there was no vision and no helper. The night seemed particularly long and the ground incredibly hard. I wished I'd remembered to bring my water skin with me. Water might ease the emptiness growing in my belly. It was in the lean-to, but I could not leave the circle to get it.

It was nearly dawn when I saw something in the grass near my circle. Peering more closely, I recoiled.

A snake!

I recognised the brown markings on its back and heard the faint rustle from its tail. It was a venomous rattlesnake! This one was not to be trusted.

As I watched, the snake lifted its triangular head and watched me with lidless eyes. It flicked its tongue, testing the air, and then with deliberate slowness, slithered towards the opening of my circle!

If I ran, I would fail the test. But if I stayed, I would be bitten by the snake.

I saw that the old dog was between me and the rattlesnake.

The snake drew closer to the sleeping dog. The mutt must have sensed something, because it yawned lazily, as though coming out of a deep slumber. Then the dog curled its tail around its bony body and went back to sleep. Why didn't the Worthless One run?

I stared in disbelief, certain the snake would bite the dog and then come for me. The rattler glided soundlessly up to the dog and I waited for the killing strike, but then something strange happened. The snake hit the dog's curled tail and stopped. It was as though the thick tail was too hard to climb over. Instead, the snake followed the curve of the furry obstacle until it was past the dog.

The rattlesnake continued towards me. It hissed and the rattles shook as it moved in for the kill.

Why had the snake bypassed the dog?

In an instant, the answer came to me. The curve of the tail had forced the snake to change direction!

Quickly, I took off my horsehair belt and laid it outside my stone circle.

The snake approached and followed the line of the belt, searching for a way in. It went past the opening, now blocked, and continued on outside the rocks. Unable to get at me, the serpent silently disappeared back into the night.

I exhaled loudly. That had been close. This far up the mountain, I couldn't have made it back to the Medicine Man in time to cut out the venom. I would surely have died.

As the sun rose, I left my sacred circle and immediately made a smudge to thank the snake for not biting me.

Then I smiled. My first night's vigil was over. Only two more to go.

CHAPTER FIVE
The Second Night

I spent the day singing and praying. There still had been no waking dream or vision and my Spirit Helper had not come to me. The sun was merciless and my thirst soon made me greedily devour the last of my water. It was not forbidden to refill my supply, but up here so high on the mountain, there were no streams. This was a serious problem. I could go without food, but I must have water.

I should not have drunk so much on the journey up the mountain. I'd been foolish. This could end my Vision Quest.

I decided to light a smudge and pray for help. It took a long time striking the steel and flint, but finally I coaxed a tiny flame in the dry sage. I was just adding a thin strand of sweetgrass when the old dog came leaping into the clearing. It stopped and shook, sending water flying into the air. The wet drops landed on my small fire, extinguishing it.

"Look what you've done!" I shouted. "You mangy dog!"

It was then that I recognised what I'd seen. The dog was dripping wet! "Where did you find water, Worthless One? Show me!" I commanded.

The dog barked once, then flopped down onto the grass. I decided to wait until it left again and then follow. Perhaps it would go back to the water hole it had found and I could refill my supply.

The afternoon dragged on and the dog showed no sign of returning to wherever it had found the water. My anger flared, but it did no good. I would have to be patient and wait.

Finally the dog stood, shook vigorously, and trotted into the bush. Grabbing the empty water bag, I followed.

The silly animal took me on a twisted route as it sniffed every tree, bush and boulder in the forest. I'd learned that shouting was futile, so I stealthily stayed at a distance, not interfering as the dog enjoyed its leisurely stroll.

The mutt trotted up to a stone outcrop, then suddenly disappeared. I followed it into a hidden cave and watched as it lapped from a trickle of water seeping out of the rock wall into a small pool.

"Ah, Worthless One, I have found your secret." I chuckled as I refilled my water skin.

"This is good. I will not have to end my Vision Quest for want of water."

Returning to camp, I happily prepared for my second night.

At midnight, the clouds rolled in and the heavens opened. The drenching rain was cold and I felt miserable. I'd had no visions, nor did my Spirit Helper come. The words of the Elder came back to me – Creator would send a Spirit Helper *if* he thought I deserved one. What if I didn't deserve a totem animal? What if I were doomed to walk my life's path alone?

Out of the corner of my eye, a shape appeared in the darkness.

I froze.

It was a wolf.

This snarling creature with bared teeth was not my Spirit Helper. It was hunting and knew I was easy prey. Again, my Vision Quest was threatened.

Behind me, I smelled a familiar odour. As I watched, the old dog padded up to the circle, raised its hackles, and began to howl. The wolf's yellow eyes flicked to the dog and it took a step back, hesitating.

I remembered hunting with my father and he'd told me how animals made themselves appear larger to scare away predators.

Stripping off my wet deerskin shirt, I stood. Being careful not to step outside the circle, I waved the shirt, threw back my head, and howled as loudly as I could. With the old dog accompanying me, our blood-chilling cries split the night.

The wolf flattened its ears and shrunk down. Turning, it fled into the woods.

"You are a coward indeed!" I laughed at the wolf, and then the old dog trotted into my circle and I ruffled the scruff of its neck. "Did you see that? I scared away a hungry wolf with no spear or knife. *I* did that!"

For the rest of the night, I sang my power song and this time I felt different, as though I deserved it.

CHAPTER SIX
The Longest Night

The next night, I was sure I would see a vision. I was also sure my Spirit Helper would come at last. My stomach rumbled as I took up my position in the stone circle, but now the hunger didn't bother me. I knew I could make it.

With a sigh, the old dog settled next to me in the circle and this time I didn't chase it away. The night was filled with smells and sounds that I'd never noticed before. There was life all around me. The air was sweet and my heart full as I watched the moon rise over the treetops. "Thank you, Creator, for the gift of this night."

Suddenly, I heard a noise that made all the terror in the world rise up and swallow me whole. A woofing sound I knew well.

It was a bear, and it was close!

Fear numbed me. I prayed the animal would pass by, but with a low growl, it lumbered into the clearing. I couldn't breathe and my hand went to the scar on my leg, as though to protect it from further harm.

The huge black bear smelled like rotting meat and I saw the long razor claws tear the earth as it hunted for grubs under a nearby log. Then, as though only now noticing, it stopped ripping at the stump and turned towards me.

I had to run! I had to hide! Could I climb a tree fast enough this time? All these thoughts flew through my mind as I tried to think about what I should do.

I'd been so close to finishing my Vision Quest, but I couldn't stay here any longer. Trying not to startle the huge monster, I prepared to leap up and run.

As I moved my hand, I brushed the fur of the old dog. I glanced down at the animal and it gazed up at me with calm eyes. It neither barked, nor moved. Instead, it held completely still and closed its eyes as though going to sleep. Was this dog crazy? The bear would have us both!

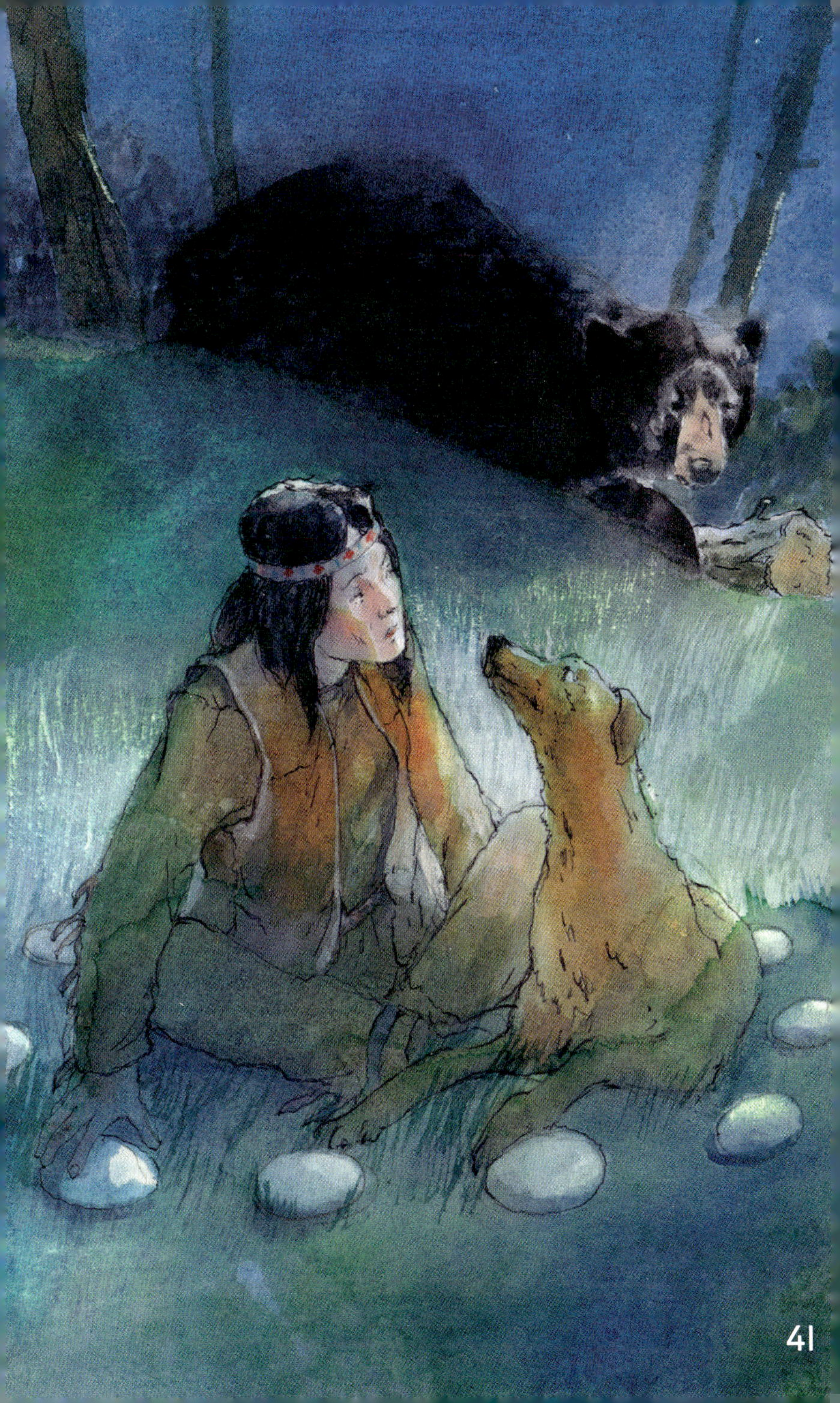

I thought of the snake and how the dog had shown me to use my belt to stop the rattler from getting too close. Then I remembered how we'd made ourselves appear larger and howled at the wolf to drive it away.

I nodded at the dog, understanding at last, and sat perfectly still. Then I closed my eyes.

My heart beat loudly in my chest as I willed myself not to move. The bear came closer and I heard it nudge a couple of my special rocks as it foraged for food.

I felt the animal's hot breath on my skin. It sniffed me, then licked the salt off my sweating face. Still I dared not move.

A huge paw nudged my leg and a razor-sharp claw pulled my moccasin off my foot! The bear chewed on the worn leather, tasting it, then spat it out and moved to the old dog.

The dog remained as still as stone.

43

Finding no threat nor easy food, the powerful bear continued past us, melting into the black shadows of the trees.

Something kept me there. I felt my fear, so deep inside me, float up and out into the cool night.

I accepted what had happened. That bear had made me afraid, made me want to run, made me want to quit, but I had not given in to the terror. I had welcomed that fear and made it my own. It had come and gone, just as the bear had come and gone.

The bear had not come to kill me. It was simply on its life journey, just as I was.

I opened my eyes to see the sun glinting over the mountain tops. Night was over. I had made it.

I stood, my muscles aching from having been still for so long. The old dog rose, shaking out the kinks in its bones. Then he looked up at me.

The deep brown eyes twinkled and I smiled and addressed the dog.

"Thank you, *Worthy One*, for being my Spirit Helper. Without you, I would have run from the bear."

I raised my arms to the sky. "Thank you, Creator, for sending me exactly the right Spirit Helper. A dog symbolises guidance and loyalty. I learned from his wisdom and he did not leave me, even when faced with terrible danger."

I patted the dog on the head. "I see now that I was arrogant. You showed me the first night we met when you laid me low in the dust." I thought of how I'd made my mother buy the trade beads for my regalia. "I must apologise to my mother for those beads. It was not about the decorations I wore, but the honour in the dance. And I should have stayed at the clearing chosen by the Elder. I'd have had water. I will remember his words as I carry my heavy stones back down the trail."

The dog made a small noise which sounded suspiciously like a chuckle.

I knelt and hugged my friend. "There is much to learn about being a true warrior and a real man, but I am not there yet. With your wisdom, I hope to be both one day."

Worthy One wagged his tail and I gathered my belongings, ready to start my new life as a warrior-in-training of the Raven People.